CHAMELEON

LIVING THINGS

CHAMELEON

Rebecca Stefoff

BENCHMARK BOOKS

MARSHALL CAVENDISH
NEW YORK

Benchmark Books
Marshall Cavendish Corporation
99 White Plains Road
Tarrytown, New York 10591-9001

Illustrations by Jean Cassels

Library of Congress Cataloging-in-Publication Data
Stefoff, Rebecca, date
Chameleon / by Rebecca Stefoff.
p.   cm. — (Living things)
Includes bibliographical references and index.
Summary: Illustrations and text provide information about the
physical characteristics, habits, and habitats of various species of
chameleons and other related lizards.
ISBN 0-7614-0118-0 (lib. bdg.)
1 Chameleons—Juvenile literature. [1. Chameleons. 2 Lizards.]
I.Title. II. Series: Stefoff, Rebecca, date   Living things.
QL666.L23S88 1997   597.95—dc20   96-1132 CIP AC

Photo research by Ellen Barrett Dudley

Cover photo: *Tom Stack and Associates*: Joe Mcdonald

The photographs in this book are used by permission and through the courtesy of:
Tom Stack and Associates: Joe McDonald, 12;Mike Bacon, 13, 27. *Peter Arnold:*
Schafer and Hill, title; BIOS (Halleux), 10 (top), Ted Schiffman, 11; Alan Morgan,
14; R. Andrew Odum, 16, 32; Gerard Lacz, 18 (left), 19 (top), 26; Kevin Schafer,
18 (right); Norbert Wu, 22-23. *Photo Researchers:* National Audubon Society, 6-7;
Gregory Dimijian, 8, 8-9, 9; J.H. Robinson, 24, 24-25, 25 (bottom); E.R. Degginger,
25 (top). *Animals Animals:* C. Dani & I. Jeske, 10 (bottom); Paul Freed, 10-11: Ted
Levin, 15; Zig Leszczynski, 17, 19; Stephan Dalton, 20-21; Richard K. LaVal, 22.

Printed in the United States of America
1 3 5 6 4 2

35, 429

To Lily Faber Muntzing

flap-necked chameleon, Malawi

retend you are walking in an African forest. What do you see in the trees?

You might see birds.

You might see monkeys.

And if you look very carefully, you might see something that looks like a small dinosaur clinging to a tree branch. Its skin is speckled green like the shadows of the leaves.

This surprising animal is a special kind of lizard called a chameleon.

Chameleons can do many wonderful things. Perhaps the most amazing thing about them is the way they change color.

In bright sunlight, a chameleon can be yellow with a few green spots. But when the chameleon runs into the shade of the forest, it turns green all over.

How long does it take you to change your clothes? The chameleon changes faster than you do. It turns from yellow to green before you can count to ten.

East African chameleon changes color as it moves from sunlight . . .

. . . to the edge of the forest . . .

to deep shade.

panther chameleon, Madagascar

Cape dwarf chameleon,
South Africa

angel chameleon, Madagascar

Parson's chameleon, Madagascar

Chameleons can wear many bright colors. They can even change from plain to striped or spotted. Some of the chameleon's changes have to do with the world around it. As the day gets hotter or colder, darker or lighter, the chameleon's skin changes color.

Chameleons also change color to "talk" to other chameleons. Bright colors and patterns warn other chameleons to stay away. And when two chameleons fight, the loser turns dull brown. This is the chameleon's way of saying "I give up."

Jackson's chameleon, East Africa

Dinosaurs? Dragons? No, these are chameleons, peering out from among the tree branches.

There are more than a hundred different kinds of chameleons. Many have horns, or tall crests on their heads, or rows of spikes along their backbones—like the ones on dinosaurs.

Nearly all chameleons live in Africa or Madagascar, a large island near Africa.

calyptratus chameleon, Arabia

anole lizard, Costa Rica

There are no chameleons in North or South America. But if you are ever in Florida or the Carolinas you may see small, fast-moving lizards that change color. They turn from brown to green to yellow or even to light blue. People sometimes call these creatures chameleons, but they are really anole lizards.

Anoles live in Central and South America, too. They are close cousins of the chameleons.

anole lizard, Peru

Chameleons have other relatives. The leopard gecko has bold stripes and spots like some chameleons, but it cannot change color.

leopard gecko, Asia

bloodsucker lizard, Southeast Asia

The bloodsucker climbs trees and changes color
like a chameleon, but it belongs to a different family
of lizard.

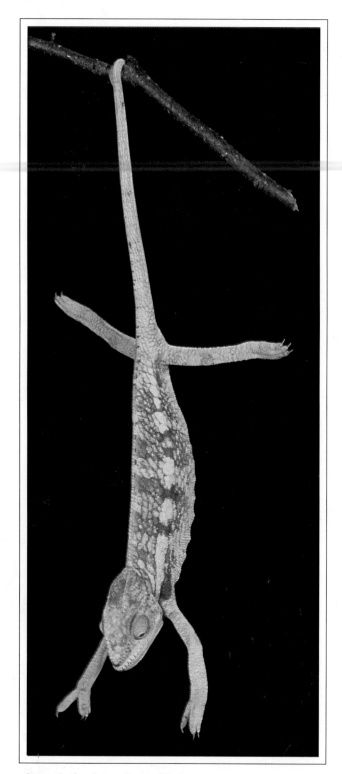

Oustalet's chameleon, Madagascar

panther chameleon, Madagascar

Whoops! Sometimes even a chameleon can slip. This chameleon has caught itself with its tail. The tail is just like an extra arm or leg. When the chameleon is not using its tail for climbing, it winds the tail into a neat curl.

Chameleons have sharp eyes. Can you look in two different directions at the same time? A chameleon can. It can watch a bird flying overhead with one eye while it looks ahead to find its dinner with the other.

flap-necked chameleon

Chameleons eat insects. But they're too slow to catch most bugs. So how does a chameleon catch its dinner?

When a chameleon sees a tasty-looking insect, it creeps close, very quietly. Then it launches its secret weapon—its long, sticky tongue. Sometimes the tongue is longer than the chameleon's whole body!

When the insect is caught on the sticky tip of the tongue, the chameleon pulls its dinner back into its mouth. Then it folds up its tongue until the next delicious bug comes along.

chameleon snatching an insect

giant banded anole lizard, Costa Rica

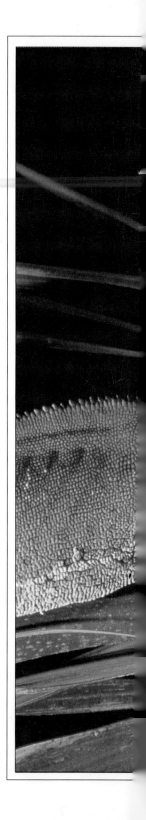

When it is time to have babies, anole lizards and chameleons use their skin to send special messages.

The father puffs out his skin and flashes his brightest colors. He wants to catch the mother lizard's eye.

When the mother lizard is ready to take the father as her mate, she flattens her body so that she looks smaller. Her stripes and spots disappear. She is saying "Yes" to the father chameleon.

female and male chameleons preparing to mate

All anoles and most chameleons lay eggs. The baby lizards use a small, sharp tooth to peck their way out of their eggs. Only a few chameleons that live high in the trees give birth to tiny live babies.

Little chameleons must take care of themselves as soon as they are born. A young chameleon can climb across anything in its path—even a full-grown chameleon!

Chameleons and anoles shed their skins as they grow. This is called molting. The old skin peels off without hurting the lizard. Underneath is a shiny new skin that is a little loose, so the lizard can grow into it.

anole lizard shedding skin, South Carolina

They're shaped like giant dinosaurs—but they're only a foot or so long.

They live in the trees like birds and squirrels—but they're lizards.

They have tails that grasp like hands, eyes that can see in two directions at once, and tongues longer than their bodies.

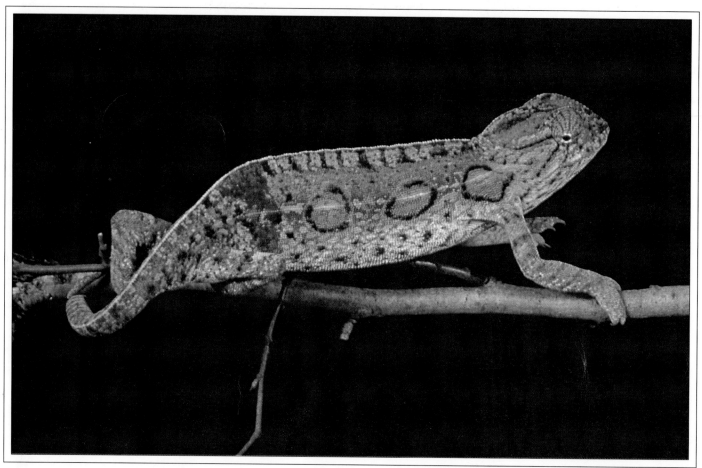

campani chameleon, Madagascar

carpet chameleon, Madagascar

They have stripes and spots and colors as bright as neon signs.

And on top of all that, they can change the way they look faster than you can change your clothes.

They are the chameleons.

A QUICK LOOK AT THE CHAMELEON

Chameleons are lizards. Like snakes, turtles, alligators, and crocodiles, lizards are reptiles. All reptiles are cold-blooded, and most of them lay eggs. True chameleons live in Africa, Asia, and the Mediterranean region. A few other kinds of lizards are sometimes called chameleons because they change color like true chameleons. These "false chameleons" are the bloodsucker lizards of Southeast Asia and the anole lizards of the Americas.

Here are six kinds of chameleons, with their scientific names and some key facts.

JACKSON'S CHAMELEON

Chamaeleo jacksonii jacksonii
(kuh my LAY oh jack SON ee ee jack SON ee ee)
Males have two horns above their eyes and one on their snout. Females have one horn or none at all. Lives in trees in East Africa. About 12 inches long (30 cm). Gives birth to live young.

EUROPEAN OR COMMON CHAMELEON

Chamaeleo chamaeleon chamaeleon
(kuh my LAY oh kuh my LAY on kuh my LAY on)
Lives in burrows in North Africa, the Middle East, southern Spain, and the islands of the Mediterranean Sea. Grows up to 11 inches long (28 cm).

CALYPTRATUS CHAMELEON
Chamaeleo calyptratus
(kuh my LAY oh kah LIP trot us)
A brightly colored chameleon with a tall crest on its head. Can grow up to 15 inches long (38 cm). The crest can be 2 inches high (5 cm). Lives in wooded valleys in southern Arabia.

FLAP-NECKED CHAMELEON
Chamaeleo dilepsis dilepsis
(kuh my LAY oh dih LEPP sis dih LEPP sis)
Males have a skin pouch under the chin that swells and changes color. Grows up to 14 inches long (36 cm). Lives in Africa from Cameroon in the west to Kenya in the east.

MADAGASCAR STUMPTAIL CHAMELEON
Brookesia minima
(brook EE zee ah MIN ih mah)
World's smallest chameleon, slightly longer than 1 inch (2.5 cm). Dull gray or brown in color. Lives among leaf litter on forest floor in Madagascar.

OUSTALET'S CHAMELEON
Chamaeleo oustaleti
(kuh my LAY oh oo STAH let ee)

Sometimes called giant or helmeted chameleon. One of the world's largest chameleons. Reaches lengths of more than 2 feet (61 cm). Eats small birds and rodents as well as insects. Lives in Madagascar.

Taking Care of the Chameleon

Some kinds of chameleons may soon disappear. Each year, people take thousands of chameleons from their homes in the wild to sell as pets. Sadly, most of them die very soon. Chameleons are also running out of places to live as people cut down the forests that shelter them. Chameleons need our protection. With our help, these rare and remarkable lizards will always be with us.

Find Out More

Hess, Lilo. *The Remarkable Chameleon.* New York: Scribner's, 1968.

Martin, James. *Chameleons: Dragons in the Trees.* New York: Crown, 1991.

Schneiper, Claudia. *Chameleons.* Minneapolis: Carolrhoda, 1989.

Index

Rebecca Stefoff has published many books for young readers. Science and environmental issues are among her favorite subjects. She lives in Oregon and enjoys observing the natural world while hiking, camping, and scuba diving.

Jackson's chameleon